Sculpting

ART TODAY!

Sculpting

Sara James

Mason Crest

Mason Crest
450 Parkway Drive, Suite D
Broomall, PA 19008
www.masoncrest.com

Printed and bound in the United States of America.

First printing
9 8 7 6 5 4 3 2 1

Series ISBN: 978-1-4222-3167-8
ISBN: 978-1-4222-3176-0
ebook ISBN: 978-1-4222-8713-2

Library of Congress Cataloging-in-Publication Data

James, Sara.
  Sculpting / Sara James.
      pages cm. — (Art today!)
  Includes index.
  ISBN 978-1-4222-3176-0 (hardback) — ISBN 978-1-4222-3167-8 (series) — ISBN 978-1-4222-8713-2 (ebook) 1. Sculpture—Juvenile literature. I. Title.
  NB1143.J36 2014
  730—dc23
                                        2014011832

Contents

KEY ICONS TO LOOK FOR:

Text-Dependent Questions: These questions send the reader back to the text for more careful attention to the evidence presented there.

Words to Understand: These words with their easy-to-understand definitions will increase the reader's understanding of the text, while building vocabulary skills.

Series Glossary of Key Terms: This back-of-the book glossary contains terminology used throughout this series. Words found here increase the reader's ability to read and comprehend higher-level books and articles in this field.

Research Projects: Readers are pointed toward areas of further inquiry connected to each chapter. Suggestions are provided for projects that encourage deeper research and analysis.

Sidebars: This boxed material within the main text allows readers to build knowledge, gain insights, explore possibilities, and broaden their perspectives by weaving together additional information to provide realistic and holistic perspectives.

Words to Understand

commemorate: Serve as a memorial to remind people of a person or event.

kinetic: Having to do with movement.

political: Related to the government of a country.

immortality: Living or lasting forever.

impermanence: Not lasting forever.

specialized: Specifically designed to do one thing.

architect: A person who designs buildings.

apprentice: A student who studies under a master of a profession.

interior design: The art of decorating the inside of buildings.

collaboration: Working together.

Chapter One

Creating Sculpture

Sculpture is one of the oldest forms of art there is. But sculpture isn't just an outdated art. Sculpture today makes life a little more interesting, whether you spot a giant sculpture in a city, have a mobile hanging from your ceiling, or are visiting a museum full of sculptures.

TYPES OF SCULPTURE

Sculpting is really just three-dimensional art. The word "sculpture" covers a lot of different techniques and materials. Sculptors have a lot of variety to choose from.

The sculpture you may be most familiar with is sculpture in the round, also called a freestanding sculpture. Old Greek and Roman statues are sculptures in the round—they stand out from anything around them and

This statue of George Washington was creating as a lasting memorial to the first president of the United States.

aren't attached to anything besides a base. Many of the sculptures you may find around cities that **commemorate** famous people are sculptures in the round.

Some artists practice relief sculpture. They start with a flat vertical surface and either carve out an image or carve out the background. A bas-relief is relief sculpture with an image that pops out of the background. Think of the way a president's head on a coin is raised up from the flat background. Sunken relief sculptures are carved into the background, so that the background is higher than the image.

Kinetic sculpture is another type of three-dimensional art. Kinetic sculptures are often freestanding sculptures, but they also move. Some kinetic sculptures move with the wind, like mobiles. Others may move if someone pushes a button or turns a gear. Some kinetic sculptures move from the force of water. Fountains are examples of water sculptures.

Assemblage sculpture is a popular form today. Assemblage sculptures are assembled; that is, they are made up of lots of different objects and materials all pieced together. Modern artists can make assemblage sculptures out of everything from seashells and beach driftwood to garbage.

WHAT'S IT FOR?

Sculpture has performed a lot of functions over the years. Some early sculptures (and sculptures today) were religious. Very early statues represented gods. People used these sculptures to aid them in appealing to gods for help. In Christianity, sculptures of saints, the Virgin Mary, and Jesus all helped tell biblical stories, since most early Christians couldn't read.

Other early sculptures were more **political**. They were created in the image of powerful kings who thought they could achieve **immortality**. Some sculptures were used to celebrate victories in battle.

Sculptures are often used as a tool to remember. Today, we erect lots of sculptures to remember famous people or events. Washington, D.C., contains many sculptures that represent great presidents, like the Lincoln Memorial, the Washington Memorial obelisk, and the Martin Luther King Memorial. Washington, D.C., also has several war memorials, like the Vietnam War and the Korean War memorials.

Cemeteries are also full of sculptures meant for remembering. Gravestone sculptures may be simple granite slabs, or relief sculptures of skulls or flowers, or tall obelisks or urns.

Sculptures, like all art, also make us think deeply about important subjects. A sculpture made entirely out of plastic recyclables found in the trash is meant to make viewers consider just how much stuff we get rid of. A sculpture made out of leaves that decay over time makes us think about the *impermanence* of our lives.

MATERIALS, TECHNIQUES, AND TOOLS

Some types of artists only use a few materials. Take painters, for instance. Painters can choose different types of paint, but there isn't a huge difference between watercolors, acrylics, and oil paint. The technique of each sort of paint is at least somewhat similar. Sculptors, on the other hand, can use just about any material in the world to create their art.

Traditionally, sculptors used materials commonly found in nature, like stone and clay. Metals have also been a frequently used material for sculpture throughout history. Other materials include wax, wood, ivory, bone, glass, ice, and sand. Sculptors aren't limited to the materials they can find in nature, though. Modern sculptors use all sorts of materials to make their art, like plastic, paper, and even electronics.

Certain materials are used for specific types of sculpture. Some people consider pottery, which is made out of clay, to be sculpture. The clay is shaped, then fired in a kiln so that it lasts longer.

Sculptures that are meant to last a very long time are often made of stone or metal. Think of the ancient Egyptians' monuments. The Great Sphinx of Egypt is one of the largest statues in the world and was built out of limestone. The statue has lasted 4500 years!

Make Connections

 Stone sculptors know that not every kind of stone is right for every job. Certain stones are harder or softer, and are more appropriate for different sorts of sculptures. Limestone, for instance, is a soft stone that carves easily but doesn't hold details very well. Marble is a lot harder, so it's more difficult to carve, but it also holds details and can be polished to a shine. Granite is another popular sculpture stone, but it is a very difficult stone to work with using normal stone-carving tools because it comes off in chunks.

There are as many sculpting techniques as there are materials, but some techniques are more popular than others. Sculptors have two basic choices. They can start with an existing material and add something to it, or they can start with the material and take something away from it. For example, a stone sculpture involves chiseling away at the stone, while creating a clay sculpture usually involves adding more and more pieces of clay to the base.

Taking away material is called carving. A sculptor may take a giant piece of stone and carve away pieces to make a stone sculpture of a person. Another sculptor may take a small piece of wood and carve away some of it to make a small wooden representation of a bird.

Casting is a popular sculpting method that has been around for thousands of years, used mostly to make metal or concrete sculptures. Casting involves making a mold, and then using the mold to create the final sculpture. First, the sculptor creates a mold out of a soft material like clay or wax. The mold is hollow so that the sculptor can then pour hot, liquid metal into it. The sculptor lets the hot metal cool into a solid.

Creating enormous sculptures like the Gardens by the Bay in Singapore required many workers, a lot of equipment, and more than a billion dollars.

She then can break off the mold on the outside, leaving the hard metal statue.

Constructing is a more modern type of sculptural technique. Constructing involves joining one or more pieces of material together using glue, pins, interlocking joints, or any number of other fasteners. Constructing allows the artist to add just about any material to the sculpture he's creating.

Different techniques and materials use different tools. Here are some of the tools artists use when making certain kinds of sculpture. Some tools are common household items, while others are very *specialized* pieces of equipment that cost thousands of dollars.

- clay: wire, sponges, brushes, scrapers, carving knives, stamps, pottery wheel, kiln
- stone: chisels, hammer, mallet, drill and bits, sandpaper
- wood: carving knives, saw, chisel, gouge, sandpaper
- metal: welding torch, welding machine, soldering iron, pliers, grinder, wire brush
- ice: saws, scrapers, grinders, chisels, ice pick, ice tongs, heat guns
- glass: high-temperature furnace, hollow steel rod, marver, tongs, annealer

Don't forget the safety equipment! Sculpture can be one of the more dangerous forms of art to create. Sculptors wear safety goggles to protect their eyes. Wood and stone sculptors wear dust masks to prevent breathing in particles of their material. Metal and glass sculptors take even more safety precautions, wearing gloves and heavy-duty aprons.

THE WHERE

Artists create sculptures in different settings, based on the type of sculpture they're creating. An artist wouldn't want to pour molten metal into a mold at home! Instead, she would probably be creating her sculpture in a studio that had special equipment and lots of safety precautions.

Sculptors who use less dangerous techniques may have art studios at home, or they might rent a studio in a community art space. Potters can make pieces at home, but they also must have access to a kiln so they can fire their fragile pieces into hard objects.

OLD AND NEW

One of the most famous sculptors of all time lived long ago, in the 1400s. Michelangelo was an Italian Renaissance sculptor, as well as a painter, **architect**, and writer. His work represents a lot of the old ways of making sculptures, including the materials and techniques he used.

Michelangelo di Lodovico Buonarroti Simoni was born in 1475 in Italy. A family of stonecutters raised him, so he learned about stone and carving very early on in life. He also liked to study the painters who decorated churches near where he lived. Because of his love of art and painting, he became an **apprentice** to a painter in Florence.

But Michelangelo was destined to be more than a painter. He soon started studying sculpture at the Medici palace. The Medicis were a very powerful family in Florence, so Michelangelo had access to all the knowledge and teaching he could want. Pretty soon he was creating professional sculptures. And all this was when he was still in his early teens!

Michelangelo's sculptures tended to imitate earlier Greek and Roman classical styles. His figures were very muscular, and often looked like the stone had aged over time even when they were brand new. His *Pieta* statue of Mary and Jesus demonstrates some of his best work. He carved it out of one piece of marble. The figures barely look like they're carved out of stone, though—the fabric, skin, and expressions of the sculpture look almost real. The *Pieta* now sits at St. Peter's Basilica in Vatican City.

Make Connections

 Usually when we think of art, we think of something permanent. A painting or a stone sculpture is probably going to be around for hundreds or thousands of years, as long as no one destroys it on purpose. However, art can also be made to be temporary. Sand sculptures, for example, only last a few hours—as long as it takes the tide and the wind to wash them away. Metal sculptures on the other hand last for hundreds or thousands of years, as long as they don't rust or are purposefully broken.

Another of Michelangelo's famous sculptures is *David*, which is in Florence, Italy. Again, he carved his sculpture out of one piece of marble. This time, it was 17 feet tall, making a larger-than-life figure.

Some artists work with students or helpers, but Michelangelo tended to work alone. By the time he died, he was a famous and much-celebrated artist.

A few hundred years later, a very different sculptor was born. Dale Chihuly was born in 1941, and he went on to become a famous glass sculptor. His works represent how many modern artists go about creating sculpture.

Dale studied art and *interior design* in college. In fact, he first worked with glass in a weaving class, and then he went to work at an interior design business in Seattle, Washington. While working there, he taught himself the very basics of glassblowing, because he still remembered how much he liked working with glass.

Research Project

Do some research to find another sculptor besides Michelangelo or Dale Chihuly, someone who has worked with a material besides stone or glass. Write a short report about him or her, including when the sculptor lived, how the sculpture discovered art and sculpture, how he or she was trained, what materials and techniques the sculptor uses, and some of his or her most famous works.

Dale decided to go back to school to learn glassblowing. He got two master's degrees and even went to study glassblowing techniques in Europe. Although glassblowing is a very old art, the sculptures that Dale Chihuly designed out of glass were very modern. He used neon colors and twisting shapes. His sculptures turned out to be as big as cars and rooms. He didn't create glass objects to be used or simply put on a shelf. He created huge sculptures to hang from ceilings.

Unlike Michelangelo, Dale Chihuly often worked as part of a team. **Collaboration** with students and other professional glass blowers was part of his everyday work. He even worked with artists who used other materials besides glass. Working with other people eventually became even more important to him when he was in a car accident that left him blind in one eye. A few years later, he had another accident that dislocated his shoulder. He couldn't hold on to a glassblowing pipe anymore. Instead of creating his works of art, he started designing them and guiding the process while other people actually made them.

Text-Dependent Questions

1. What is the difference between a bas-relief and a sunken relief sculpture?
2. Give three reasons people create sculptures.
3. What are some of the oldest materials artists have used to create sculptures? What are some of the newest?
4. How does the construction type of technique for making sculpture work?
5. Name at least three tools used for making sculptures out of wood.

In the later part of his career, he and his team created sculptures that looked like giant Christmas tree ornaments floating in water, huge chandeliers, and glass gardens. Dale Chihuly helped make glass into a modern art form of sculpture.

Words to Understand

fertility: The ability to produce children or make life grow.

ceramics: Sclupture made of clay and hardened with heat.

indigenous: Coming naturally from a certain place.

terracotta: A brownish-red clay used for pottery and sculptures.

idealized: A perfect representation of something; better than in real life.

traditional: The way things are usually done or have always been done.

found objects: Regular items that an artist finds and uses to make art.

Chapter Two

The History
of Sculpture

Sculpture has a very long history—almost as long as the history of people, in fact. Sculpture is one of the oldest art forms, along with painting. Just about every society all over the world has made some sort of sculpture. Covering the entire history of sculpture is no easy task!

PREHISTORIC

Sculptures were an early way to communicate, before writing was even invented. We don't know a whole lot about prehistoric sculpture, but a few examples have survived. The most famous is the Venus of Willendorf,

Olmec sculptures of enormous heads like this were created more than three thousand years ago.

found in Austria. The tiny Venus is 25,000 years old and carved out of limestone. The sculpture is of a round woman, who represents *fertility* and life. She is an example of an early religious piece of art. The Venus of Willendorf is just one of many fertility sculptures people have found around the world.

Other prehistoric sculptures have been found carved into figures of horses, rhinoceroses, lions, birds, and other animals. Most are made out of stones, while some are carved from wooly mammoth ivory.

All prehistoric sculptures that have been found so far are small. People moved from place to place, following the animals they hunted. They had to be able to carry everything, including their art works, with them.

INDIGENOUS AMERICAN

Small groups of people have lived in the Americas for thousands of years. The Olmecs were one of the first big civilizations, centered in what is now southern Mexico. The Olmecs created large stone heads around their empire. One head could weigh as much as 40 tons! The heads might be images of rulers or warriors.

Other Olmec sculpture included smaller stone sculptures. A few were made out of jade, a bluish-green stone. Some figures were creatures that were a mix of jaguar and human. Wood and ceramic were also popular materials for Olmec sculptors.

The Olmecs passed their art on to the major civilizations in the Americas that came after them, like the Aztecs. Sculptures of huge gods sat in ancient Mexican temples and other public places. Men and women praying, animals, and plants were other popular subjects. Many Aztec sculptures were made of stone like basalt and jade. Some were *ceramics*.

Later examples of *indigenous* American art include the totem poles of Northwestern native tribes in the United States, which were built over the past few hundred years. Totem poles were made of tall, straight tree trunks carved into figures and shapes. A pole told the story of the person who had the totem pole built, including the family history, how wealthy the person was, and what he had achieved in life.

AFRICAN

Early Egyptian sculptures are some of the best examples of ancient art. A lot of the sculptures were focused on life after death. Pharaohs built giant tomb sculptures—the pyramids—to commemorate their lives and to prepare for their deaths. The tombs inside had stone statues that represented the pharaohs and other nobles, along with Egyptian gods. Tombs also included smaller sculptures of ordinary people and relief sculptures of everyday scenes. The smaller sculptures were meant to

This mask of King Tut was one of the sculptures discovered inside his tomb.

offer the pharaohs their services in the afterlife, depending on what the sculpture was doing. Women grinding corn and scribes who could write down messages were common figures.

The fact that Egyptian sculptors used stone and could create such large and detailed sculptures shows that the ancient Egyptians were a powerful and enduring presence in that part of Africa.

In western Africa, the city of Ife (in present-day Nigeria) was another site of great sculpture. In the twelfth to fifteenth centuries, sculptors made *terracotta*, brass, and copper statues of heads, masks, and figures. The sculptures are very detailed and lifelike. They portray a wide range of normal people, from the elderly to royals to the ill.

In much of Africa, wood has been the most popular material for sculpture, because it's so abundant, unlike other materials like stone. Early wooden sculptures don't exist today, because they have rotted away, but more recent examples are still around. Wooden sculptures from the southern half of Africa represent ancestors, gods, and royals. Wooden masks were used in religious ceremonies or for chiefs to wear.

Make Connections

King Tutankhamen was actually a very minor Egyptian pharaoh. He ruled in the fourteenth century BCE for only nine years. He didn't do a whole lot while he was ruler, but he is one of the most famous Egyptian kings today because his tomb was never robbed over the thousands of years since his death. Most other pharaohs' tombs were cleared out of statues and other things, but explorers discovered King Tut's tomb fully intact in 1922. Some of the things inside the tomb were a throne, gold statues of the pharaoh's head, animal sculptures, boats, and more. It was one of the biggest Egyptian sculptural discoveries ever made.

Roman sculpture was meant to portray real people as they actually looked.

EUROPEAN

The Greeks had the first big civilization in Europe. Like other early cultures, the Greeks sculpted gods and other religious symbols. They sculpted in stone and in bronze. Stone statues of gods and goddesses were put in temples, which were places were people could worship. Ancient Greek sculpture is very lifelike. Sculptors spent a lot of time detailing muscles, postures, and faces. The Greeks made a lot of sculptures in their day. For example, there are hundreds of sculptures decorating the inner and outer walls of the Parthenon temple in Athens.

The Romans took over the Greek Empire. They adopted the Greek style of sculpture, but they added their own artistic touches. The Romans liked to use sculpture to tell stories. The Column of Trajan in Rome has a strip of bas-relief sculpture that tells the story of a victorious Roman war. Many Roman sculptors focused on portraits, portraying real people as they actually looked, rather than *idealized* versions of people. Sculptures decorated tombs, gardens, public spaces, and private hallways.

When Christianity took over Europe, sculpture wasn't a big part of the new religion. Early Christians thought it was wrong to use sculptures or paintings of people and gods to worship, so sculpture didn't really have much of a place.

However, after about a thousand years of Christianity, Christian sculptors started to create new works. Architecture techniques improved, and people were able to build bigger and bigger churches. Painters and sculptors decorated their churches with scenes from the Bible, demons, angels, animal figures, plants, and people. This first phase of Christian art and architecture was called Romanesque, because people used old Roman art and buildings as inspiration.

Next came Gothic sculpture. Like the sculpture that came before it, Gothic sculpture was mostly used in churches for religious purposes. During this period, sculptors got better at portraying realistic-looking figures. They made tall, thin sculptures, which reflected the tall, airy Gothic churches in which they were housed.

The next phase of European sculpture was the Renaissance, which means "rebirth." The Renaissance started in Italy in the fourteenth century as a way to revive Greek and Roman traditions. During the Renaissance, sculptors continued to create art for religion. They also sculpted rich people, horses, tombs, and fountains, among other things. Renaissance sculptures were very serious and dignified. Michelangelo and his stone sculptures—along with his paintings—is one of the most famous Renaissance artists.

Immediately after the Renaissance, the Baroque style of art became popular in Europe. Baroque art, including sculpture, was more playful, involving illusions and drama. The sense of movement was important, and many sculptors incorporated the moving water of fountains into their works.

ASIAN

Asia covers a vast area, so its sculpture is varied. Some of the earliest Asian sculpture comes from the western part of the continent, from what is now the Middle East. Mesopotamia was one of the first human civilizations in the world. Along with writing, cities, and farming, ancient Mesopotamia had sculpture.

Mesopotamians didn't have access to lots of stone, so sculptors used materials like clay and wood. Sculptures tended to represent religious figures, like gods and people worshiping the gods. A little later on in history, Mesopotamian sculptures show kings and warriors, as the society became more warlike.

Other parts of Asia also had sculpture. On the Indian subcontinent, sculptors in the Indus Valley (modern-day Pakistan) created small pottery, bronze, and stone figures. After that, not many sculptures were made in this region until artists began to use sculpture to depict religious scenes from Hinduism, Buddhism, and Jainism. Emperor Ashoka, for instance, had 85,000 Buddhist temple sites (called stupa) built in the mid-200s BCE, to spread the religion around India. As Hinduism became more important, more statues of Hindu gods and goddesses appeared.

Buddhist art also made its way into China. In one place called the Longmen Grottoes, caves contain thousands statues of Buddhas and Buddhists. A recent study that tried to count them all came up with 142,289. China has a long history of sculpture, from ceramic pottery to tombs complete with thousands of statues. The tomb of Shi Huangdi contains more than six thousand terracotta life-size soldiers standing guard over the king.

OCEANIA

Hundreds of large and small Pacific islands make up the region we call Oceania. People on these islands have been creating sculptures for thousands of years, just like people everywhere else in the world.

Early sculptures from Oceania included artistic baskets. Later on, sculptors began to create wooden carvings. Wooden sculptures adorned masks, boats, and bowls.

The island of New Guinea in particular has a long sculpture tradition. Early stone sculptures of figures are common there, and so are decorated mortars and pestles, which are used to crush and grind food. The mortars and pestles are carved into reliefs, and have bird or human heads on them.

On Easter Island, huge stone sculptures called moai stand looking inland to the island. They represent different chiefs of the people who lived on Easter Island. People today still can't quite figure out how the stones were carved and transported to their sites, because they're so large and weigh so much. It's a mystery!

MODERN

For most of sculpture's history, artists had created figures of gods, people, or animals. Modern sculptors were interested in moving beyond

Research Project

 We often learn a lot about Western art—art that is directly influenced by European ideas and beliefs, and less about non-Western art. Choose one of the many examples of non-European sculpture periods presented in this chapter and research it more fully. For instance, you could choose to search for more information on the life-like sculptures of Ife, or the Northwest Native American totem poles. Write a paragraph about what the sculpture was like, including a description of the final product, the materials it was made out of, and the techniques used to make it. Then write a paragraph or two about what it was used for. Finally, write at least a paragraph about the historical context of that type of sculpture. Why did it develop? Was it influenced by art that came before it? Did it influence art that came later?

the *traditional* subjects, to new ones. They wanted to use sculpture to explore things like ideas and emotions.

Modern sculptors also turned to materials different from the traditional stone, clay, metal, and wood. They used plastic, steel, and *found objects* instead. Construction became an important sculptural technique. Before, most sculptors had carved out their art, but now, artists began to piece it together a bit at a time.

It's almost impossible to come up with a description of modern sculpture. Every sculptor has a different style. Some stick to realism and create sculptures of real-looking people, animals, and objects. Others make abstract sculptures that only suggest objects, or aren't even meant to represent objects at all.

Many modern sculptors stretch the definition of sculpture, bringing it to new heights. Christo and Jeanne-Claude were a husband and wife

Text-Dependent Questions

1. What were prehistoric sculptures used for? Why were they so small?
2. Why did Egyptian pharaohs hire sculptors to decorate their tombs?
3. To which period of European sculpture did Michelangelo belong?
4. What were early Mesopotamian sculptures used for?
5. How do modern sculptors challenge the artistic traditions of the last centuries?

team who created very large-scale sculpture installations of fabric, which spanned whole buildings or even counties. They wrapped buildings in fabric, surrounded islands with fabric, and covered Japanese hillsides with blue umbrellas.

On the other hand, Andy Goldsworthy creates smaller sculptures that were meant to disappear after a few hours or days. He makes spirals out of brightly colored leaves and ice, balances rocks, and arranges sticks into caves. The only materials he uses are ones found in nature, and many blow away or melt after a little while; only the photographs of the sculpture endure.

As you see, sculpture has a long, varied, and fascinating history. People have been using sculpture to express themselves for thousands of years. But they have also used sculpting as a way to support themselves. Sculpture has been and continues to be a career choice for many artists.

Words to Understand

professional: Someone who does something to get paid.
cooperative: An organization of people who work together
to help each other.
commissions: Money paid to artists to create custom works of art.
flexibility: The ability to do many different things.
supplement: Add to or complete something.
auctioneers: People who sell art or other items at an auction.

Chapter Three

The Business
of Sculpture

Sculptors aren't just artists—they're businesspeople too. Sculptors have to make money if they want to dedicate their lives to making sculpture without spending time on other jobs.

Artists of all kinds usually find it hard to break into the business. Sculptors need skill, determination and hard work, some money to get them started, and some luck. Becoming a **professional** sculptor isn't easy, but for some people it's a rewarding and worthwhile career choice.

There are lots of different sculpture businesses out there. Most sculptors focus on trying to sell their works to individual people or companies.

A potter may work with other potters, so that together they can help each other sell their work.

Some sell at arts-and-crafts shows, while others have their own galleries to show and sell their art.

Sculpture business also depends on the type of sculpture being created. An ice sculptor might offer her services to catering companies who are providing food and entertainment for large events. Or that ice sculptor could try and get hired directly by people and companies planning big events like weddings and holiday parties. A potter, on the other hand, might join a pottery *cooperative* and sell his work at a gallery with lots of other potters who are also displaying their work.

WHO DO SCULPTORS WORK FOR?

Most sculptors work for themselves. They own their own businesses, and they either make sculptures to sell to customers, or they take *commissions* from clients who want specific sculptures made. They work on their own time to create their own work. Working for themselves offers them the most *flexibility*, but can be hard for sculptors just starting out who aren't making very much money, and who aren't well known.

Some sculptors work for other people. A sculptor might work for an interior design company, creating freestanding sculpture when a client would like one. Or a sculptor just starting out might work for another sculptor, helping to create her pieces.

A few sculptors end up as teachers. Some, particularly very successful ones, will be offered positions in colleges and universities, teaching fine art. Others teach high school or primary school sculpture or general art classes, and still others teach community sculpture classes. Teaching is a good way to *supplement* the work that sculptors do creating their own pieces of art, since it provides more income and contacts with potential customers and other art businesspeople.

GETTING PAID

In 2012, the U.S. Bureau of Labor Statistics showed that the average income for all professional artists was $44,850. That includes people who

Creating wood sculptures requires a great deal of skill. Some people do it as a hobby—but sometimes what starts out as a hobby can lead to a business, when people begin to commission work.

Interior designers sometimes use original sculptures when they create one-of-a-kind living spaces.

make less and those who make more. The lower end of the pay scale for artists was $19,410 while the higher end was $93,030.

Of course, there are the few sculptors that become famous and make lots of money, but they're the exceptions. Most sculptors don't become particularly rich, but many end up making enough money to live comfortably. Some sculptors also have second jobs, which they work at full or part time. When they become more successful, they can quit their jobs if they want, to focus solely on sculpture.

Sculptors who create works with metal and glass need special equipment. They may work alone in studios or share space with other sculptors.

Make Connections

 Sculptors usually work in some kind of studio. Lots of sculptors have their own studios at home, or in a group studio space. A sculptor who creates small clay sculptures might have a space at a pottery studio. A wood sculptor might have a home studio set up in his garage. Sculptors who work with metal or glass have to have special equipment that isn't normally found in the average studio! Glassblowing involves a large glass kiln, special benches and safety equipment, and torches. Very successful artists might have their own studios, while others who are just starting out share studio space with other metal and glass sculptors.

Having a second job as a sculptor doesn't necessarily mean giving up on sculpture. There are some jobs that deal with sculpture and art that don't directly involve creating sculpture. Artists work in art supply stores or warehouses, museums, galleries, and as *auctioneers*. Second jobs can actually help sculptors get a better understanding of the art world and get more contacts that can help their businesses grow.

A SCULPTOR'S CAREER IN ACTION

In an interview with The Art Career Project, metal sculptor Bruce Gray explained that he was always interested in sculpture, since he was a kid. He started building things as early as first grade, and he made his first artistic sculpture in middle school. Later on, he took woodworking and metal shop classes in high school, and in college, he earned a Bachelor of Fine Arts (BFA) in design.

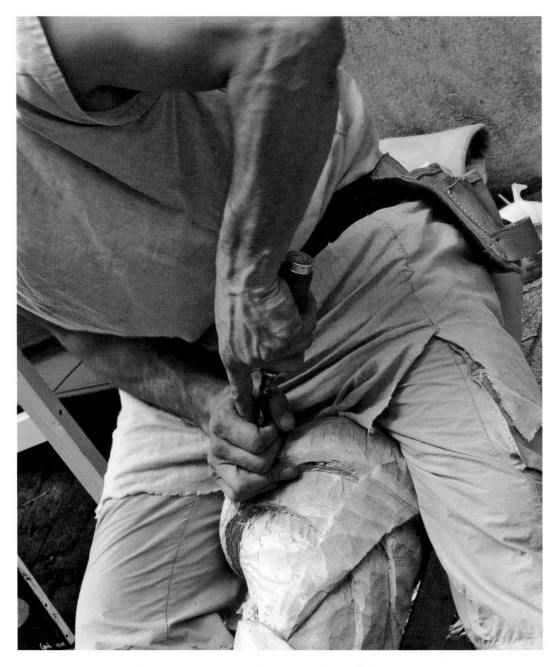

Creating sculpture often requires physical strength that wouldn't be necessary for other forms of art.

Deciding to sculpt full time was a scary but fulfilling decision for Bruce. He said, "I graduated from the University of Massachusetts in 1983 and worked for a few years in photography and graphic design in Boston. I was not sure if I could leave a job with a regular paycheck and make a living as an artist, but decided it was what I wanted to do most with my life. I have always been a hard worker and good with tools, so I just jumped into the art world full time and went for it. I had no idea if this would work, but you only go around once in life."

Bruce worked hard at getting his name out there. To start off, he decided to try and sell his sculptures to furniture stores, which would sell them to their customers. He also sent out postcards to local businesses, to convince offices to buy his art as decorations. Bruce's marketing paid off, and he now has a thriving business.

Bruce didn't rely on just one method of growing his sculpture business. His long list of practices includes, "going to art openings, sending out postcards, working with galleries and museums, participating in charity events with art auctions, exhibiting at art fairs, advertising, sending out press releases on your best new sculptures, hanging out with other artists, moving to an artist community, and having a website. Social media like Facebook, Youtube, and having your own blog can help a lot too." He finds customers at art gallery openings, through his own gallery showings, from his website, and by word of mouth.

Although not all sculptors are as lucky or as successful as Bruce Gray, he proves that it is possible to work your way up in the art world. He started with raw talent and a university degree, and then worked hard at marketing himself to be able to sell his sculptures.

STRUGGLE FOR SUCCESS

Becoming a sculptor and creating a sculpture business is never easy, but it's harder for some people than others. Augusta Savage was a black

An ice sculptor has to accept that her work isn't going to last!

Augusta Savage in 1938 beside one of her statues.

woman who pursued a sculpture career despite the obstacles in her way, including racism and sexism. She's a great example of how hard work can lead to a successful business, even in the face of the worst barriers.

Augusta Savage was born in 1892 in Florida. She started sculpting when she very young, making animal figures out of the clay she found in the ground. Her family wasn't very supportive, but she kept on sculpting. She even won a prize at the county fair. Then Augusta started selling her sculptures locally, though her first efforts to set up a business failed financially.

Research Project

Do some research to find another sculptor who was either black or a woman (or both). Write a short report on that person's art and the struggles he or she faced because of racism or sexism. If the artist you chose is still alive, try and find some interviews with her to learn about her experiences in her own words.

To pursue her career, Augusta moved to New York City and went to Cooper Union for college. The school didn't charge tuition, and it gave her some money she could use to pay for things like food. While she was at Cooper Union, she applied for a summer art program in France. She was rejected because she was black, and she couldn't change the minds of those who were in charge of admittance.

After college, she kept on sculpting in New York City. She set up her own business as a portrait sculptor. She was so talented that she was commissioned to create sculpture portraits of W.E.B. DuBois and Marcus Garvey, important African American leaders of the early twentieth century.

In the 1920s and 1930s, she finally traveled around in Europe, studying art and creating sculptures. When she came back to the United States, she started teaching sculpture and created her own art studio to help younger artists—particularly African American ones—get started in the business.

By this time, Augusta was well known. She created a sculpture called

Text-Dependent Questions

1. Who might a sculptor work for, if he's not working for himself?
2. What is the benefit of having a second job as a sculptor?
3. According to the sidebar in this chapter, where might sculptors work? What are some of the factors that determine where they work?
4. How did Bruce Gray market himself to grow his sculpture business?
5. What were some of the art businesses that Augusta Savage set up?

The Harp for the 1939 New York World's Fair. The sculpture was a harp that also included singing African American figures. She couldn't afford to cast the plaster sculpture in metal, so *The Harp* ended up being destroyed.

Augusta tried to set up a small art gallery for African American artists, and she held her own small gallery showings. She never made enough money to keep her efforts going, though, so she eventually retired to the Catskill Mountains in New York. Today, though, her work is still remembered, and it still inspires other artists. Augusta proved that success means more than just a lot of money!

Words to Understand

custom design: Make something to match your needs and wants.

templates: Designs that have already been made in advance.

Chapter Four

How Can I Get Involved in Sculpture?

I f you think you might be interested in being a sculptor, now is a great time to start exploring the business. By planning ahead when you're young, you have a head start on success.

TAKE CLASSES

If your school offers art classes, start taking them if you haven't already! Many schools have a class completely dedicated to sculpture. Take any art classes you can, even if sculpture isn't one that your school offers. Getting exposure to art in general will help you with whichever type of art you decide to make your specialty.

You might also be able to find community art classes. Larger towns and cities sometimes have education centers that offer classes in things

Working with clay can be a good way to get started with sculpture. Many communities offer beginning pottery classes.

Creating works from glass takes specialized skills and materials. Some communities offer glassblowing classes, and most art schools will offer classes in glass.

like dance, music, computer skills, and maybe even sculpture. Local art museums may also have similar programs.

Think ahead as you make your college plans. Many sculptors have an advanced degree in art. A Bachelor of Fine Art (BFA) is especially helpful. Taking a few years of art classes gives students access to teachers with a lot of knowledge, along with advanced equipment and tools. Many artists discover and refine their artistic style while in school.

Different colleges offer different sculpture courses, but students at art colleges typically have plenty of choices. If you attend an art school, you could take mold making and casting, stone carving, ceramics, figure modeling, glassblowing, and more. Some schools specialize in one sort

Museums sometimes employ sculptors to help repair statues and create replicas.

of sculpture, so if you know you want to go into pottery, for example, you can find schools with good ceramics programs.

START PRACTICING

Even when you're taking sculpture classes, or in your time outside class, practice sculpting! Experiment with different materials to learn things from each, and to find what you really like to work with. Play around with Legos, wood, fabric, and anything else you can think of using.

While some people might be more naturally talented at art and sculpture than others, everyone, even the most talented people, needs to practice. Honing your talents over time will help you become the best sculptor you can be, no matter where you start out. Practice builds up your creative skills too!

START YOUR OWN BUSINESS

Sculptors don't follow just one path. Some end up creating artistic pieces sold at galleries, while others sell at arts-and-crafts fairs and anywhere else they can find. You can decide which path you want to take based on what kind of sculptures you make, how much time you have to dedicate to your business, and your own personal preferences. You might not have time to dedicate yourself to a full-time sculpture business as a young person, but you can start planning ahead or even start a part-time business if you feel like your sculptures are good enough to sell.

Diving right into a business without a roadmap is almost never a good idea. Deciding to start a sculpture business doesn't mean you'll just be creating sculptures all day, every day. You have to spend a lot of time developing your business and then marketing it. To start off, you'll need a business plan, which provides a guide for your business. You can always change it later, but a business plan helps you figure out what you want your business to look like right off the bat. A business plan should include:

If you're interested in sculpture as an art form, play around with it whenever you have a chance. Experiment with different materials. Be creative!

Make Connections

Small business owners need to get a license to legally open their business and start selling to customers. Photographers mostly have to worry about local licensing at the town or city level. Check out your city's website to figure out how to get a license. Usually it involves a small fee and some paper work, and isn't a big deal. In a few cases, the city doesn't require that some small businesses get a license.

- Summary. If someone doesn't have enough time to read the whole plan, he can just read the summary to get a quick overview.
- Objectives/goals. Why are you starting a business, and what do you hope to achieve with it?
- General company description. Write down your mission (the reason your business exists), your form of ownership (like sole proprietorship, limited liability company, or corporation—you can find out more about these by talking to an accountant or lawyer), customer audience, and business strengths.
- Industry description. What does the sculpture industry look like right now, and how do you fit in?
- Product/service description. Explain what sort of sculptures you'll offer, and how much you'll charge for your work.
- Marketing plan. You'll need to know how you're going to advertise or otherwise get people to know your business.
- Competition. Who will you be competing with in the business world? What makes you stand out?
- Distribution. Make sure you know how you'll get your sculptures to your customers. Will they pick them up? Will you deliver them?

It can take a lifetime to build a successful career as a sculptor—but if sculpting is something you love, it could be a satisfying and exciting path.

A craft fair can be a good place to get some practice selling your sculptures.

Business plans make running businesses a lot easier. People with plans have figured out what they want out of their businesses. They have more than vague ideas; they know what their businesses will look like. That puts them a step ahead of everyone else.

After you've written your business plan, you'll need to start putting the plan into practice! You'll probably need a little money to buy some tools or advertise your business. Remember, start small, especially if you're still improving a lot as a sculptor, and if you don't have a lot of time to

Sculpture will always be more than a business. It's a way to express what is most important to us, a way to show the world something new.

Some sculptors are employed by animation studios, to create the clay people and creatures that seem to move on the screen.

dedicate to a business. You can start saving up your own money, or ask for small loans from family members who might want to help you out.

MARKETING

Even if you have amazing sculptures that you're sure people will love, your business won't take off if no one knows about it! Spend some time marketing your business and your sculptures.

Marketing involves getting the word out about who you are and what you do. Think about where your potential customers are. For example, are you trying to sell to other young people? Then see if you can advertise in your school newspaper, or post flyers around your school or

Stonework is a specialized form of sculpture. It's often used in outdoor settings, so landscape design companies might be good places to market this kind of sculpture.

Research Project

Do some more research on small business plans and see if you can find a useful template that makes creating one a little easier. Create a short plan for a part-time sculpture business you would be able to start as a young person. Make sure you include all the important information, and edit it to make it look as professional as possible. Make up some things if you have to, based on what you'd like your business to look like. This is just for practice!

places where young people like to hang out. Tell your friends about your business, and encourage them to tell their friends.

It's also a good idea to have a portfolio of your work. Portfolios are large folders with pictures of the art an artist has created, although sometimes portfolios can be stored solely online or on a flash drive. When you're visiting a potential customer, you can take out your portfolio and show him your work. He might see something he likes and ask you if you can create another piece like it. You've made a sale!

To have a successful business these days, you also need to market online. Having a website is really important, along with a Facebook page, and maybe a Twitter account and LinkedIn profile. People will probably find out about your business through your website or through social media. If they hear about you from a friend by word of mouth, they'll want to check out your business online first before deciding to hire you.

Your website should have lots of examples of your work. Potential customers will want to see the types of sculptures you create. If you have many different styles of sculpture, you'll be able to introduce people to

Text-Dependent Questions

1. Where might you be able to take sculpture classes if your school doesn't offer them?
2. What sort of college degree do many sculptors get before they become professionals?
3. Name at least four sections a business plan should include.
4. What is a portfolio, and why is it important?
5. How can you use your website to grow a sculpture business?

your entire collection. If someone sees one piece you've created, they can visit your website and see even more examples. Maybe they'll even decide to buy one, if your website offers your work for sale or points customers to where they can buy them offline.

If you know how to design a website form scratch, great, but there are plenty of options for people who don't. Wordpress, Wix, and Tumblr are all good options. They let you **custom design** your own site from **templates**. You can include all the information you need, plus lots of photos of your sculptures.

Remember, if you're starting a sculpture business, you need patience. Starting any business isn't easy, and art businesses can be especially hard. Jumping into the art world can be scary, but it can also be exciting! If you love to sculpt, you're joining a very long tradition of sculptors stretching from prehistoric times to the modern sculptors of today. So pick a style, start practicing, and don't give up!

Find Out More

Online

100 Greatest Sculptures Ever
www.visual-arts-cork.com/greatest-sculptures-ever.htm

Biography.com: Famous Sculptors
www.biography.com/people/groups/sculptors

International Sculpture Center
www.sculpture.org

Sculptor.org
www.sculptor.org

U.S. Bureau of Labor Statistics: Fine Artists
www.bls.gov/oes/current/oes271013.htm

In Books

Brown, Claire Waite. *The Sculpting Techniques Bible: An Essential Illustrated Reference for Both Beginner and Experienced Sculptors*. Edison, N.J.: Chartwell Books, 2006.

Emert, Phyllis. *Pottery (Eye on Art)*. Farmington Hills, Mich.: Lucent Books, 2008.

Mariotti, Steve. *The Young Entrepreneur's Guide to Starting and Running a Business.* New York: Times Books, 2012.

McNeese, Tim. *Michelangelo: Painter, Sculptor, and Architect.* New York: Chelsea House Publishing, 2005.

Nardo, Don. *Sculpture (Eye on Art).* Farmington Hills, Mich.: Lucent Books, 2006.

Series Glossary of Key Terms

Abstract: Made up of shapes that are symbolic. You might not be able to tell what a piece of abstract art is just by looking at it.

Classical: A certain kind of art traditional to the ancient Greek and Roman civilizations. In music, it refers to music in a European tradition that includes opera and symphony and that is generally considered more serious than other kinds of music.

Culture: All the arts, social meanings, thoughts, and behaviors that are common in a certain country or group.

Gallery: A room or a building that displays art.

Genre: A category of art, all with similar characteristics or styles.

Impressionism: A style of painting that focuses more on the artist's perception of movement and lighting than what something actually looks like.

Improvisation: Created without planning or preparation.

Medium (media): The materials or techniques used to create a work of art. Oil paints are a medium. So is digital photography.

Pitch: How high or low a musical note is; where it falls on a scale.

Portfolio: A collection of some of the art an artist has created, to show off her talents.

Realism: Art that tries to show something exactly as it appears in real life.

Renaissance: A period of rapid artistic and literary development during the 1500s–1700s, or the name of the artistic style from this period.

Studio: A place where an artist can work and create his art.

Style: A certain way of creating art specific to a person or time period.

Technique: A certain way of creating a piece of art.

Tempo: How fast a piece of music goes.

Venue: The location or facility where an event takes place.

Index

About the Author

Sara James is a writer and blogger. She writes educational books for children on a variety of topics, including health, history, and current events.

Picture Credits

Fotolia.com:
6: Laiotz
8: spiritofamerica
12: jo
18: Paweł CYGAN
20: Rafael Ben-Ari
22: Christopher Dodge
24: Andrea Izzotti
30: Mi.Ti.
32: Forster Forest
34: dobri71
35: Photographee.eu
36: Scott Griessel
38: Food photo
40: ponsulak
44: Krzysztof Wiktor
46: lunamarina
47: Andrea Izzotti
48: Pavel Losevsky
50: Africa Studio
52: Forster Forest

53: Ingo Bartussek
54: monamakela.com
55: marcovarro
56: Daniele Pietrobelli

41: Archives of American Art